At the Pond

Comparing Numbers

Jane Gould

Consultants

Chandra C. Prough, M.S.Ed.
National Board Certified
Newport-Mesa
  Unified School District

Jodene Smith, M.A.
ABC Unified School District

Publishing Credits

Dona Herweck Rice, *Editor-in-Chief*
Lee Aucoin, *Creative Director*
Chris McIntyre, M.A.Ed., *Editorial Director*
James Anderson, M.S.Ed., *Editor*
Aubrie Nielsen, M.S.Ed., *Associate Education Editor*
Neri Garcia, *Senior Designer*
Stephanie Reid, *Photo Editor*
Rachelle Cracchiolo, M.S.Ed., *Publisher*

Image Credits

p.6 Design Pics/Newscom; p.9 iStockphoto; p.18 Vasyl Helevachuk/Dreamstime; p.22 (frog) Photowitch/Dreamstime; p.23 (snail) Kryozka/iStockphoto; p.27 (snail) Kryozka/iStockphoto; All other images: Shutterstock

Teacher Created Materials

5301 Oceanus Drive
Huntington Beach, CA 92649-1030
http://www.tcmpub.com
ISBN 978-1-4333-3430-6
© 2012 Teacher Created Materials, Inc.
BP 5028

Table of Contents

What is at the pond?

There are 2 frogs.

There are 7 bugs.

7 is **greater** than 2. There are **more** bugs than frogs.

What is at the pond?

There are 2 newts.

There are 5 turtles.

5 is greater than 2. There are more turtles than newts.

What is at the pond?

There is 1 raccoon.

There are 8 ducks.

8 is greater than 1. There are more ducks than raccoons.

What is in the pond?

There are 4 fish.

There are 2 snakes.

2 is **less** than 4.
There are **fewer**
snakes than fish.

What is at the pond?

There are 5 snails.

There is 1 dragonfly.

1 is less than 5.
There are fewer
dragonflies than snails.

What is in the pond?

There are 10 lily pads.

There are 3 flowers.

3 is less than 10.
There are fewer
flowers than lily pads.

What is at the pond?

There are 3 hawks.

There are 3 otters.

3 is **equal** to 3. There is the same number of hawks and otters.

What is at the pond?

There are 6 worms.

There are 6 tadpoles.

6 is equal to 6. There is the same number of worms and tadpoles.

What is at the pond?

There are 2 beavers.

There are 2 birds.

2 is equal to 2. There is the same number of beavers and birds.

There are more fish than turtles.

10

2

There are fewer flies than frogs.

2

9

The number of ducks and snails is equal.

5

5

How many toads are at the pond?

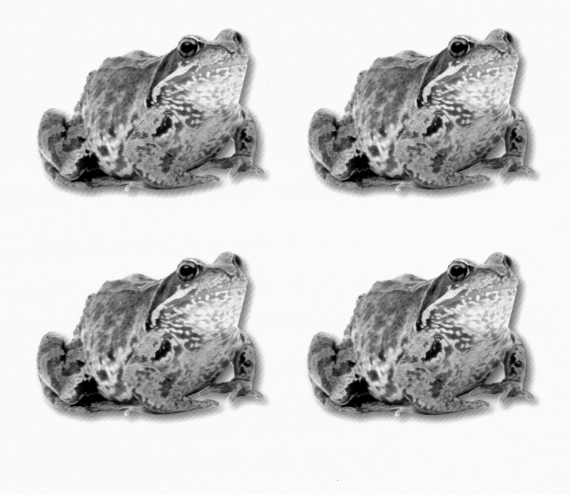

1. Point to the equal number of toads.

2. Point to the greater number of toads.

3. Point to the fewer number of toads.

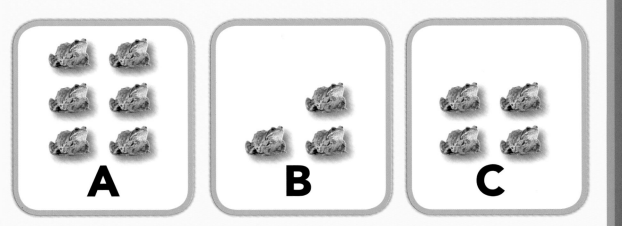

A

B

C

Count the animals.
Which type has more?
Which type has fewer?

Which animals show an equal amount?

Who has more?
Who has less?

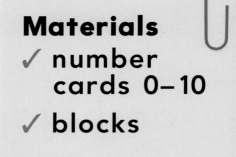

Materials
- ✓ number cards 0–10
- ✓ blocks

28

1 Work with a friend.

2 Pick a number card.

3 Count out the number of blocks and stack them.

4 Who has more blocks? Who has less?

Glossary

equal—the same amount

fewer—a smaller amount

greater—a larger amount

less—a smaller number or amount

more—a larger number or amount

You Try It!

Page 24:
4 toads

Page 25:

  1. C

  2. A

  3. B

Page 26:
more fish; fewer snakes

Page 27:
dragonflies and ducks

Solve the Problem

Answers will vary.